Animal Senses

Heather Hammonds

Contents

Rigby

A Harcourt Achieve Imprint

www.Rigby.com
1-800-531-5015

Our Senses

We have five senses.

We can see,

smell,

hear,

taste,

and feel things.

Animals have senses, too.
The senses help animals
to find food
and stay out of danger.

hear

see

smell

taste

feel

Lion

Look at this lion's eyes.

The lion's eyes help it

to see in the dark.

The lion is looking for food.
It can see lots of animals
in the dark.

Owl

This owl is sitting in a tree.
It is looking for a mouse
to eat.

An owl has big round eyes
to help it see at night.

Anteater

An anteater has a long nose to help it look for food. This anteater is looking for some ants to eat.

The anteater can smell
ants with its long nose.
It will dig down
into the ground
to find the ants' nest.

Snake

A snake can taste
and smell things
with its tongue.
This snake is looking
for food.

The snake puts its tongue
in and out.
It smells the air
and finds some food.

Rabbit

A rabbit has very long ears that help it to hear.

A rabbit can move
its ears around.
It will run into its **burrow**
if it hears a fox.

Octopus

An octopus has **suckers** on its arms.

It can feel things with its suckers.

The octopus
can hold onto things
with its arms.

Glossary

burrow

suckers